WHICH WAY TO LOOK

Also by Susan Hauser

Meant To Be Read Out Loud
What The Animals Know

WHICH WAY TO LOOK

by

Susan Hauser

Loonfeather Press

Published by Loonfeather Press
426 Bemidji Avenue, Bemidji, Minnesota 56601

Cover design and graphics by Roger Winters

Printed in the United States of America
First Edition

ISBN 0-926147-03-X

This publication is made possible in part by a grant provided by Region 2 Arts Council through funding from the Minnesota Legislature.

Acknowledgements

These essays were written for and broadcast on KCRB Public Radio, Bemidji, Minnesota.

Some of these essays have also appeared in A *Merrie Prairie Christmas, Anna's House, Loonfeather* and *Country.*

CONTENTS

3

Which Way To Look

January is a quiet time for most of us. The stream of company that crests at Christmas is dried up, friends and relatives returned to their own hearths to wait out the cold. We hunker down too, making no plans to travel. We turn instead to that which is at hand—things we can touch and carry from room to room: a book, some needle work, paper and pencil—things we can work our fingers into the way time reaches into our hearts and makes a little stir there.

And when we want company, we turn to each other. At the kitchen table our hands flutter over gaming boards: backgammon, Scrabble, Wykersham, Pente, chess. Waiting for our turns, we hold game pieces in our hands, feeling that tiny warmth that comes from things not alive themselves, but somehow giving back the life we bring to them.

In between, we sit sometimes at the same table and just look outside at the world. Once in awhile we try to conjure the larger globe, the places we see on the evening news, but new snow that rises off the lake and hangs itself in drifts in the yard precludes any sense we might have of masses. For as far as we can see, as far as we could yell, there is no human breath but ours.

Only the birds come in flocks. They fill the trees with their color: pine and evening grosbeaks, redpolls, purple finches. And halfway down the hill, on the last elm tree left standing, the topknot of a pileated woodpecker flicks in and out, a ruby beacon against the grey and white backdrop of this season.

I have been watching this bird for two weeks now. I understand why it is sometimes called the lord god woodpecker. As long as my forearm, it hangs itself from the elm bark and has-at the wood with its fine, long bill. Its shoulders are muscular. Its back tapers down through white markings to tail feathers strong as a spine and braced against the tree, absorbing the hammer blows. Wood yields that is too hard for humans to split.

On the side of the tree that I can see, one beaten out trench is three feet long, four inches wide and four inches deep. It makes a jog to the right half way up, then goes straight again. Another trench above it is a foot long. Another one starts above that, the hole still a circle, an eye into the secrets of the heartwood.

At the foot of the tree a pile of wood chips grows, a little mountain, a tribute to persistence. From this distance, I try to read the hieroglyphs of the scars themselves, but I cannot make out the words.

Closer to home, the chickadees come and go from the jugs of seeds I've hung from the tree nearest the house. Nuthatches also dash in and out, as though they had to steal. Downy and hairy woodpeckers forage at the suetstation. Sometimes I do not know which way to look: close to home, at these birds that feast with us like family, or down the hill to the pileated woodpecker, alone at its task, gleaning food from a tree we thought was bereft of life.

The Storm

All day we wait for the storm. It is predicted. It is coming up from Texas and across Kansas and Iowa. It will even find us in our northwestern corner of Minnesota.

People did not always wait for storms this way. Before radio and television, changes in the weather were announced by the presence of clouds, the heaviness of the sky, and the smell of the air.

I wonder if it is instinct that makes me watch for signs of the storm while we wait for it. The sky is overcast, but the clouds seem far, far away, high in their own heaven and unconcerned with earth. I certainly do not know how to read weather, but even I can see that the forecast is wrong. This storm is not going to get to us. Like some human ambitions, it must have faltered along the way, dissolved in a passing wind, or taken a turn in a different direction.

We fill the wood box anyway, and check the cupboards and fridge to see if we should make a quick trip to town. As yesterday's footprints glimmer in the last of the shrouded sun, we stand in the window and comment on the obvious: this time we will be passed by. Our words do not speak of disappointment, but our voices do.

It is special to be snowed in. The demands of ordinary life are lifted, and time no longer matters. Schedules are wiped out with the same thoroughness as tracks covered by blowing snow. Grownups and children stop to look at each other and wonder what to do during this time-out from the twentieth century.

The evening, we think, will remain a common one. We eat in the early dark, pick up our nightly pleasures, books and knitting, and turn on the television. But sometime in the hours between work and rest, something in the dark outside the window begins to move. The wind comes up a little. We sense it before we really hear it.

I turn on the outside light. The wind grabs and tosses the wind sock on the flag pole. The snowmen in the yard take on new postures: snow that was coming in sideways from the north wraps itself around them like scarves.

We stand again side by side at the window. Down the slope at the edge of the yard we can see the faint outlines of the old barn foundation. Jenny, who used to live here, told us once about lambing during a blizzard. She stayed all night in that barn, with only a lantern and the heat of birth for warmth. Roland had not returned from town. There was no telephone. She only hoped that he had seen how ripe the clouds were and had not tried to come home, or had stopped along the way to spend the night with strangers.

We stoke the fire, turn off the outside light and return to our chairs, but now things are different. We are getting snowed in. We get to stay home. Can't go if we want to. Can't go if we have to. The promise and the threat rub against us like a coarse blanket, both keeping us warm and reminding us of how cold it can be.

Mirror, Mirror

I wake slowly, thinking the cardinal calling up the dawn is singing in my dream. But as I become aware of the light in my room, I remember that I am not home in Minnesota. I am in Florida. Like the summer birds, I have fled south from the winter.

I turn toward the window and read across the sky and trees the way we skim a book sometimes. The angle of the sun is different from home, and the leaves on the tree outside my window move differently. They bump about rather than shimmer. As I realize that in fact there is no breeze at all, the shadows I am watching suddenly lift into flight—it's now a flock of sparrows. They settle back into the tree just as quickly, becoming restless leaves again.

The morning air is soft and ethereal, but I rouse to the smell of coffee slipping up from the kitchen downstairs. At the table, I sit in silence with my brother and his family. The birds at the feeder are telling all there is to say, and we are content to stare at the lake, its mirrored surface as blank as our morning minds.

The bell that rings us back to sound is not human-made. We all vocalize at once when the mirror breaks and the blue-black back of an alligator slices along the water.

A second back surfaces. Through the binoculars we watch them move along the way cows graze in a meadow, their iridescent backs glinting in the sun and their eyes intense with knowledge. They disappear finally in the tangle of vines that have captured the shore of the peninsula across the way.

We finish breakfast, all of us awake now, but we have been touched briefly by life that is deeper and stronger than ours, and we want more. We fill our coffee cups and head down to the lake. Nick makes a snake-checking tour of the pontoon boat and we all climb aboard. Snakes. We have them at home, but only harmless "garters" and "ribbons." As the boat eases away from the dock, serpent shapes move all around me: the gas line, control cables, piping on the boat cushions.

Nick nudges the boat along the shore and then turns in a wide circle toward the peninsula across the way. Water vines tremble in our slight wake, and I let myself be rocked by the motion of the boat.

Then it is there, ahead of us and to the left, its warty back decorated with vines, like a child playing camouflage. Nick stops the boat, and we all stand silently and stare. I am embarrassed. This creature only wants some sun. As though the weight of our eyes is finally too much to bear, it slaps its way back under the water's surface. The vines close over the space where it had been.

We float awhile in water as quiet as death. We watch around for a ripple where our prey might be surfacing again. Nothing. We have only his disdain to treasure.

We do not go right back home, but loop around the long-fingered points of land made out of the dredgings from the phosphate pit that preceded this lake. It is more than twenty years since the mines were active, and the goddess flora has reclaimed her land: the branches and leaves of ferns and vines and trees tangle with each other like wind-blown hair. A turtle slips off a half-sunken log. Like the 'gator, it too is allowed passage in the Edenic underworld. A water turkey follows us from bay to bay, flying a little ahead, as though it knows before we do which way we will go. A great blue heron, cousin to the ones that nest near my Minnesota swamp, stays put on its chosen branch and watches us glide past.

I am glad when we finally slip into the berth of the dock and it is only land that separates us from the house. We went out to investigate the wildlife, but came back being the ones found out.

Seed Catalog

One advantage of living in the country is that you have to go outside to get your mail. No matter how lazy you feel, or how bad the weather is, if you want to know what the postwoman has put in that little tin house, you have to abandon the stale, staid air of home and set yourself out in that other somehow truer air.

Knowing there is mail in the box is for me like a ringing telephone is for some people: I have to respond to it, have to go out to the road, even if it is twenty-five below with a good wind blowing.

This mid-winter day I am doubly glad to have been rescued from my own indolence. A south wind last night has pulled snow from the yard and hung it out in little windrows from the snowbanks that line the driveway. My eyes dazzle in a high, bright sun, and the scene at my feet is a miniaturized polar landscape.

I have entered a fairy world. Overhead, a squirrel objects to my presence, its noontime task of scattering seed casings on the fresh snow interrupted. To my right, a pileated woodpecker stops its rattatattat and moves itself around to the other side of the tree.

The hiatus is brief. I arrive at the mailbox and find there is excitement inside: a newsprint page sticks out from the bottom of the stack of mail, revealing the tips of a handful of bright green bean pods and a tumbling down pile of blood-red strawberries.

A seed catalog. I stuff the first class mail into one parka pocket, my mittens in the other and walk back up the driveway guided by habit, looking not at my feet, but at the wondrous spread of color and promise that I hold open in my hands.

At the kitchen table, I set out pencil and paper, sip tea and begin to plan. French Breakfast radishes. Candy Pack carrots. Mr. Society hybrid yellow onions. The garden is buried under two feet of snow, but I know where I will put each treasure. I draw circles for the squash hills, long lines for rows of corn, an X for the bean trellis.

And we do not live by vegetables alone. I turn to the flower section. Super Majestic Giants Colossal Mixture: the aristocrat of all hybrid pansies. Giant Royal sweet peas. Everblooming Bouquet flowers. On my paper, I draw a dotted line where I can spade up the sod and make room for more beauties. This year I will add roses: Nocturne, Mr. Lincoln, Mr. Whiskey. Never mind that the map says hardy in Zones three-ten and we are stuck up here in Zone two.

I wonder sometimes about the madness that strikes a person exposed to a seed catalog in January. Maybe it's a side effect of cabin fever. Or maybe there is something in the ink, or in the truer-than-life photographs. The little map I am drawing has no room for weeds. The pictures of the glistening jars of pickles do not show the pillar of steam rising from the canning kettle into the August heat. The boy sitting on the hundred pound Big Max pumpkin does not have to roll it up the hill to the house.

Maybe it is the position of the sun in the sky that lets fancy rule over fact. That haymaker is only now beginning to make real headway toward us. The afternoon light is still slant and catches

12

in the crystalline facets of the snow. The snow itself seems utterly permanent. Perhaps summer is just a dream we had once. There was hot sun, and cool shade, and tomatoes grew with the ease of grass and ripened with the speed of dandelions. There were no chores, only the delicious task of the harvest, and winter seemed as benign as gardens do in January.

Walking On Snow

Today we go out walking on snow. That is not anything like walking on water, of course, but it is liberating. So far, the deep snow of this particular winter has kept us on the paths to the bird feeders and the duck house. We should have snowshoes, but we don't, and our skis have been useless. They won't climb the wind packed drifts, and as light as they are, they are too heavy to lift over and over again through a foot of new fluff.

But yesterday the snow melted a little, and last night it refroze onto itself. Like the actual surface of the earth, it formed a solid crust that is strong enough to hold a human. Our feet do plunge through now and then, throwing us to our knees or sitting us down where we had been standing, but that is no different than a walk through any day, when events or emotions or ideas we are sure of suddenly give way beneath us. We do the same thing then as we do now: we pull ourselves up with as much dignity as possible, try to be a little less sure of ourselves, and to read more accurately the surface we tread.

Our venturing out today is driven by more than pleasure: it is nearly spring, and is time to prepare for making maple syrup. Last fall we pulled the summer's windfall branches into piles about the yard. Today we will begin to pull them over to the sugaring arch.

We skid our way over to the sugar bush, east of the house, and separate, to locate our energy hoards. I plant my feet in front of one, grasp one of the branches holding itself out from the snow like a hand, and tug.

It does not move. I try another. Frozen. Frozen solid. Frozen tight. Frozen stiff. I look over at Bill. He is arm wrestling with a thick, grey limb. I scan the grove, looking for encouraging signs. Nowhere does wood rest on top of snow. In the grip of last fall's golden weather, we forgot about the grip of snow.

We join up, and continue our walk around the yard, poking and kicking at the piles of sticks. Our conversation is a bouquet of cliches: What were we thinking of? What's the matter with us? When will we learn?

"At least we are not as bad as the dogs," I say. We make our way over to their part of the yard, forty square fenced in feet. They come over to talk to us, dancing a little on top of the snow and resting their chins on the top wire of the fence. They still haven't figured it out, I marvel. They are peering over the top of a six foot barrier. They have not noticed that the snow has raised ground zero three feet or more. They could step over into freedom.

"Maybe they don't want to," my husband says. "Maybe they like their life the way it is."

"I don't know," I say. "It seems like the ultimate denial." But I have had enough of lessons for one day. I inch along the fence until I get to my bird feeder path, a narrow spine of snow that I know will hold me up if I stay true to it. I put my arms out for balance, keep my eyes on my feet and follow my own footprints back to the house.

Accidental Garden

I love to watch the dragon flies. In the country where I live, they are big four-wingers, the semi-trucks of the dragon fly family. All day in June they work the air around the house. Their legs form little baskets and they plow from one end of the yard to the other, gathering mosquitoes and gnats. Like the rest of us, they seem to have a territory for which they are responsible. They go back and forth, back and forth, little cleaning ladies of the sky.

How can a bug be both a semi-truck and a cleaning lady? In June everything is possible. Weeds blossom and become flowers. The symphony of the frogs that in May signals the end of winter in June turns cacophonous, and instead of opening the window by the bed, I close it.

And this year I have two accidental gardens in addition to my planned one, the one outside the west kitchen window, the garden I have worked on for six years. In the spring, it gives me more than a hundred tulips and daffodils. One day I had eight bouquets of flowers in the house, and the garden was still full. Then the poppies turned on, and now the sundrops are about to ignite.

In fact, this garden has grown so well that I have had to cull it. Two years ago I moved some of the iris to a patch out near the field. I confess to being a recycler, a nice word we use these days for a hoarder. Maybe someone will want some iris one day. I can give them some from my storage garden.

I forgot those iris, and last year with the drought, they stayed low in the grass, keeping their own council. This year they revived, and last week, they came into bloom: a stand of butter-yellow flower heads waved from above the grass and an accidental garden was born.

As I rip weeds from the little pathway of my intentional garden, I like thinking about that iris out there on the edge, where grass and fallen limbs and animal trails encroach on our tentative grasp on this land. I like that the earth is at least as diligent as human beings when it comes to survival.

My third garden lies between the other two. It is outside the south kitchen window. When we bought this place, the lawn had spent a season in summer fallow. Without the leveling blade of a mower hacking off its every effort, a small stand of day and tiger lilies emerged right through the sod. We cut around it the first year, picked grass around it once in awhile after that.

Then we began to enjoy the hardy determination of this spontaneous plot. One year we added an apricot tree seedling. When we found roses trying to get ahead of the grass out by the mailbox, we brought them in to this friendlier turf. This year I put in a little blue creeping flower that I got from a lady at a garage sale. Like the dragon flies, we keep grazing over the same little bit of land, sprucing it up, making it ours for the few moments that we give it our attention.

Sometimes I wonder which garden I like best: the one I planned and keep in order, the one that holds its own out on the rim of things, or the one in between, that has grown the way our dreams do, a little at a time, and not quite the way we thought they would.

It is like trying to choose a favorite friend, or food, or place to be: the answer depends on the moment itself, on which window I am looking out of, and whether it is a day in June and the dragonflies are cruising.

There's No Place Like Home

I am at home now, at my desk, looking out at the long northern Minnesota marsh that feeds from our south fence line into Mud Lake. I had always thought of the swamp as colorful—red and yellow willow switches sweeping the ground, verdant canary grass trailing its tresses and evergreens lifting against the sky. Today it is different: I see a black and white snapshot, innocuous and slow. I have just returned from Hawaii.

It was dark when we landed in Kona. House and street lights lifted like stars against Mauna Loa and Mauna Kea, two of the five mountains that form the Big Island. Grateful to be on the ground after more than eight hours in flight, I leaned back as we drove up the mountain to the home we would visit. The car swayed gently from left to right, around one curve, then another, up one slope, then another. We would drive this road dozens of times in the next two weeks. This first passing, in blissful dark, would be the only easeful one.

In daylight I became a white-knuckle passenger. All of the island is a mountain slope. At every turn, no matter how far we drove, the sea was off to one side, its surf a thin white line against the black lava shore. From the lanai on the west side of the house, it was a thing of beauty. From the back seat of a car gripping the outside of an unrailed curve, disaster loomed from every angle.

Back at home the swamp blends gracefully into the treeline across the way. The ebb of the epicontinental sea that washed here over three million years ago has left no echo. Even the more recent glaciers that scooped out this meadow and deposited our hill seem but distant mammoth landscapers that politely withdrew when their work was done.

The land was set down and the land remains. Wind and rain only scribble on the surface. There is always a firm place to put your foot down, to say "this is mine." A mountain does not stand for that. It is omnipotent and omnipresent.

Hawaii is a vacation mecca not because of the color and warm seas, but because when you are in Hawaii you are nowhere else. Your brain is there, your eyes, your nose. Even your heart, when it is not in your throat or your stomach. The first morning we were there, the echo of my office phone went dead. There was only a cardinal whistling up the morning, doves and myna birds chortling and a mongoose ransacking the fruit fall outside our window.

At least the flowers are silent. But if their color does not take over your eyes, it is because your eyes are fixed, out of necessity, to your feet. Unless you are going to stay within the hotel grounds, leave your little white sandals at home. Bring tennies, rubber thongs, anything with a sole that can hang on to ball-bearing lava. With every step you take on a Big Island path or beach, you will feel the mountain's sovereignty. We went up to Kilauea, home of Madame Pele, Goddess of Volcanos. Drove across lava less than five months old. Walked around sulphur vents, our throats and lungs cringing. Dante knew his stuff.

We stepped over fissures in the earth, stuck our hands into steam vents that poured forth the hot passion of the earth's core. I do not like to know how easily earth cracks apart. Hawaii is a full color moving picture, seen from the front row. If that is paradise, it is one made for fools.

Nature's Revenge

Mid-July already. Blueberry time already. Anticipation fills my head the way leaves fill the trees in August.

At the gas station the other day someone said indeed, the blueberries are ripe. That night I called a friend who frequents the woods. He thought not—still little green B.B.'s when he was out the other day.

The only way to tell for sure is to go look for yourself. I call another friend. Armed with pails and insect repellent, just in case, we mount the pick up and ride off to check out the blueberry fields.

As I turn off the county road onto a grass-packed woods trail I announce to my companion that we probably will not be picking in this spot, even if the berries are ready. "Poison ivy," I explain.

I didn't think I would have to say more. "Can't you wash it off?" she says.

Some people think so, and in fact you can, if you have a water tap or running stream within reach. The insidious oil can bond with the skin within ten minutes. Depends on the person. Depends on the skin. Depends on the amount of oil.

"Don't count on it," I say, and stop the truck across from the crumbling homestead foundation that still guards the dual track of this old road.

We get out to inspect the berries, and to teach poison ivy to Helen. Standing respectfully back, as though the oil could leap from the glossy leaves to my susceptible skin, I point to a robust example. The three leaves shoulder their way above the blueberry plants and young hazelnuts. "Three leaves, always," I say. "Sort of wavy around the edges."

"They're beautiful," Helen says. "I hear the Indians didn't get it because they ate the leaves."

"Indians got poison ivy." Everyone gets poison ivy if they live long enough. I know. I thought I was immune. I'd scrounged in woods all my life and never got it. I felt pretty smart about it too. Then a few years ago I helped a friend clear sumac off her hill.

"There's poison ivy down there," she told me. "That's all right," I said. "I'm not allergic. Besides, my skin is covered. And I'm wearing gloves." I proceeded to spend a half hour scootching around on the steep hillside, nipping off sumac and thoroughly crushing poison ivy leaves and berries into my jeans, which I continued to wear for several days more.

It was a week later when the backs of my upper legs began to itch. By the end of the day they were aflame, and within two days they looked like I had raked them with a wire brush. I washed my jeans, but it was way too late. I had poison ivy.

Like all first-timers, I tried an unending list of home remedies, though I eschewed bathing in horse urine and treating the sores with sugar of lead, a guaranteed cure, according to an 1896 government pamphlet. The rubbing alcohol and hydrogen pyroxide and calomine and cortisone cream kept me occupied, and offered new hope when

I thought the only appropriate response was filleting the backsides of my legs. When we had house guests I told them if they heard weird moans of satisfaction coming from behind closed doors, it was only me giving in to the passion of temporary relief by scouring the backs of my legs with a fingernail brush.

Sticking to the path that still holds the memory of wagon wheels, Helen and I mosey along deeper into the woods, stooping now and then to pick small red thimbles of wild strawberries that dot the grass. Mark was right. The blueberries are not ready. The only harvest we will take home today will be oil of *rhus radicans.*

I don't know what Helen is thinking about as the pungent forest air and subtle woodland sounds saturate our talk, but I know I am transported somewhere else: to the laundry room at home. I have an image of feeding everything from my toes to my neck into the wash machine, then dashing to stand under the cool waterfall of the shower while offering up a meditation, half prayer, half threat, that will guide every drop of nature's greatest revenge down the drain and into the sewer and back into the dark cave of earth from whence it arises.

Cruising Down the River

We enter the canoe with the grace and silence of a flock of sea gulls, if three people constitute a flock. The man from the resort points us in the right direction and gives us a little shove, releasing us to the water and the walls of trees and banks that line this part of the Mississippi River. The current, he promises, will do most of the work, and in about four hours we will appear at the lakeside of the resort, where we have left our wallets, our car keys, our car and, we hope, the noise of our normal lives.

The river is low, even with the drawdown from the dam just above us. In fact, it is quite a bit lower than three weeks earlier when I made this journey with my other sister. That time, when the water gave up on us, only Karen had to get out and walk, guiding the canoe along side of her, and wondering out loud why I got to be Katherine Hepburn and she had to be Bogie.

This trip the water gives out on us almost right away and even Kate Hepburn ends up walking for the better part of an hour.

"Aren't you glad to be out here on the river, away from the frustrations of city life?" I ask my big sister Gretchen, and her husband. They are visiting from Houston, and are happy that the nights are cool, and that the daytime sun is forgiving.

"This is wonderful," says Gretchen, letting her state of the art running shoes pick up the rhythm of walking in water. In just a few minutes she learns how to read the ripples on the surface and the colors below the surface, and is moving through the multi-sized rocks with the agility of a great blue heron.

Little fish dance around her ankles. In the water just ahead, rafts of ducks paddle and dabble, always keeping the same distance between us and them, as though a wedge we cannot see is placed firmly between us.

Eventually there is enough water, and the canoe skims along first with one passenger, then two, then three. By the time Larry is in and shaking the sand and water out of his Reeboks, the river has taken hold and for a long time the current does carry us.

At first it seems utterly quiet. We cannot hear traffic, or other people, and find ourselves whispering. But as we become more silent, the land we travel through becomes louder. We hear as well as see the water as it collides with the glacial rocks that are everywhere. The ducks that seem to move and feed like mimes actually slurp and burble and emit duck-chatter that sounds like a radio left on in a distant room. A pileated woodpecker concealed in the woods releases heart-startling reports as it hammers into a tree.

We begin to feel at home. Nature is not so different after all and we are not in the closed sanctuary of a church. As the doors of our hearts swing open we settle into conversation and song. Most of the time, the river does indeed carry us along, but sometimes we have to paddle, forcing our way through seaweed rafts, or insisting that our craft take a different channel than it is inclined to.

Toward the end of our little journey the river opens up into swamp. The current falls far below us along the bottom of the water course, the way the direction of our lives sometimes dips out of view, and we move ahead by a combination of momentum and force. The sounds of the water and woods are replaced by the conversation of tall grasses. We stop talking then, and Gretchen and Larry pull their paddles hard against the steady weight of the water and I, sitting in the middle, close my eyes, my head lifted.

Then we are out on the lake. Human voices and motors fill up the spaces we had made empty. I do not mind. The pleasures of the day are settled into my bones, the way silt settles on the river bottom. We will go home now, taking on the jackets of our lives, but anytime I want to, I can reach down into the river, and stir the waters.

Richfield

I grew up in Richfield, Minnesota. Anyone looking at a map now would call it a suburb of Minneapolis, although it is a city in its own right. When I lived there it was technically a village. I didn't know that, of course. Government boundaries are of no use to children.

We drew our maps with different lines: St. Martin's backyard, Newquist's driveway and the abandoned dirt road behind Colbert's house. We called it Crookety Lane. It was our access to Wood Lake, a small, mud bottomed slough hemmed in by hills and cattails and canary grass. It was there we learned about boundaries. They were clearly recorded, not on paper, but in our hearts.

At Wood Lake, we hid from strangers, from each other, and even from ourselves. We learned about small deaths there, when the land that was, after all, wilderness yielded up the corpses of birds and mice and fishes.

And we became friends there, singing down the sun and walking home close together, the glow of our certitude holding back the impending dark.

I liked the clarity of that miniature world. When scrutinized, it revealed internal depths: the shin bone of a shrew, a snail's trail along primeval slime. But I was called too by the world up the hill, the one with streets that had names and led one way to open fields and the other to the city.

It was my grandparents who showed me those streets. On Sunday afternoons, they came and got me and drove me away from home. I sat in the back seat, rubbing my hands on the maroon velvet. We scouted for land. My grandfather was a builder of houses. He built the one I lived in, and the ones over on Diamond Lake Road. We drove over there sometimes and scanned the yards.

But most of the time we headed straight for the country. The houses thinned out and finally disappeared. Fields took over, rich fields, and the sky became longer and wider. The sun hung high forever and sometimes I wondered if we would ever go home.

Every childhood is interrupted by the coming of age of the human body. I was doubly wrested from youth. The year I was thirteen, we moved. Still, it was anti-climax. The year before, Patty's parents had taken her away, and Kippy's took her the year before that. Only Lottielee and Diane remained. None of us had been down to the lake for a long time.

For another, longer time, I forgot about Wood Lake. I followed the streets my grandparents showed me, paths that went farther away than any of us imagined they could. Finally, I went back to visit.

Riding in from the airport, I drove by houses nailed to land I remembered as fields, glowing and golden in Sunday sun. And I went to Wood Lake. Now it is a nature reserve, drained of its center by the dry life of the city, and gathered inside the folds of a chain link fence. I walked in there. Grasses grew where water had been.

I had changed too. I sat a while then, on a bench on a boardwalk that reached to the middle of the lake bed. Ducks had come down once right where I was sitting. I closed my eyes, heard the quiver of their wings as they conned their landing. It matched perfectly the beating of my heart.

Dancers

As the car drops down the slight hill toward my uncle's driveway, my heart rate picks up a little. The street seems not to have changed in all the years I have come here, the only home I remember for Joe, and the only home left from my childhood.

For a moment I feel how tenuous our hold on property is. In this old neighborhood, where pines and oaks have all they want of the sky, tricycles and bikes, dropped along the sidewalk like stones, betray the lives of younger families. City plots, like forests, cycle through different kinds of growth, each one yielding predictably to the next.

I turn into the driveway and pull up short in front of the weathered garage door. Even the outside of this house bears the seal of the past, but once inside, I am scooped up into the arms of the present: kisses and hugs from Joe and Georgia, chatter and talk about today and tomorrow.

It is not until we sit in the dining room for lunch that history leans into us. Over the table, a circle of lights hangs from the ceiling. From it two tiny dolls, a man and a woman, each one the length of my little finger, dangle on opposite ends of a foot long thread. It is looped over one of the golden arms of the light fixture and six inches down the dolls hang free, moving in the air currents. The last time I saw this miniature couple, they were draped over the carved oak leaf on the clock on Grandmother's shelf. She would not let us touch them, but she liked to take them down and show us how they danced. I did this now. I stood up from the table, and lifted the dolls off the golden hook and held the middle of the string between my thumb and forefinger. The dolls turned a little, settled back to back, their arms perpetually reaching out, one leg of each kicked back a little, ready for the dance.

With my other hand I pulled the woman doll away from the man and then released her. Predictably, she caught one of his outstretched arms and they twirled together in a little spin. The string climbed itself as far as it could, then held the dolls still for a moment, then let itself go, and the dolls danced the other way around. They caught and released and caught each other again and again until the breath of the string ran out and they settled again against each other, moving only with the rhythm of my breath as it rocked my hand.

I sat down with them, held them in my open palm, and as I looked and looked at them, the detail of the dress came back to me. I remembered the finely wrapped threads of their legs and arms, the minutely crocheted clothes and coiffures. the little lines of their faces.

I like to think they came from Germany, maybe with Grandmother's mother, pulled out from a pocket during a long voyage, their familiar little dance bringing momentary comfort to a journey with a dubious end.

"You remember them?" said Joe.

"Yes. They were Gram's. She made them dance for me."

"You may have them."

I made them dance again. "They are too precious. You should keep them."

"No, I want you to have them."

I held them again in my hand, cradled them, as though to still a crying.

As though hanks of thread could carry love through long years.

As though Grandmother's arms could reach out from yarn dolls and catch me in a little spin.

Uncle Joe reached over and caught my hand in his. We danced then, in our hearts, the thread of time turning to our turning.

Stepping Out

I awaken slowly in the strange room. My eyes come into focus on the net of stuffed animals hanging directly over the bed. My first thought is of those rafts of balloons they use at rallies and concerts. They hover over the crowd until just the right moment and then the right strings are pulled and, fleeing like children from school in the afternoon, the bright colors shake themselves free of each other and seek their own places in the sky.

This net of animals, though, released would drop right onto my face and chest. This is the right image for children, I think: fuzzy and dirty and capable of overwhelming a not quite awake grownup.

I sit up a little, just in case the net is stretched beyond its limit but has not realized it yet, and look further around this child's room. It belongs to my husband's grandson. My stepgrandson, an awkward tag for a twelve year old, and one we do not bother to use. He is Kael. I am Susan.

We are friends. This visit, I helped him make his hallowe'en costume. We giggled and fussed in the basement, pressing bright stars onto his Merlin cloak, rummaging under the workbench for stiffener for his magician's hat, and sitting together on the bottom step when our legs were so tired from holding us up over the ironing board that we couldn't stand it for one more star.

For Kael this was an adventure in costume making, and it was for me too. He thought I knew what I was doing, didn't know I made it up as we went along. Didn't think about the faking-it training I'd had with my own two children. Didn't know how echoes of their gestures and complaints bounced back at me from the cold concrete floor, and lodged under my breastbone.

Toward the end, we made concessions—fewer stars on the belt, a long wrinkle not pressed out. Kael was eager to get his treasure up to his room, to hide it from his brother, he said, but I think he wanted to be alone in his private place, to dress, to be Merlin, to be magic. He was beginning to sense that all was not easy in this world. A good costume couldn't hurt.

The sleight of hand had worked for me. Under the gilded moon that we heat-fused to the tall cone of the hat, my own small children, absent in fact, became present in heart. When Kael went to his room, I let myself outside into the generous cool air. There seems to be more room for grief in the presence of the sky.

There is no room at all for grief in the presence of children. I was setting myself up for a good cry, when the other stepgrandson materialized next to me. Yes, I was going for a walk. Yes, he should come along.

We set ourselves onto the side road that would not take us anywhere. "I've just learned how to walk," I announced, as we picked up our stride. "Do you want to learn?" Dusty is ten. He thinks I am wonderful. I told him how to hold his hips forward and as he thrust them into the void ahead of us, his skeleton locked into place and he moved ahead like a ship underway.

Amazed, he stopped, turned and looked at me. "It works!"

"I know," I said. "Isn't it funny that we can learn to walk all over again, when we've been doing it for years?"

We both put our hips forward and let them lead us down the pavement, zooming by the little plants we usually stopped to talk about, and ignoring the birds that peeped at us from the bushes. We were on our way, striding into the rest of our lives, our arms swinging in tandem beside us.

Walking that way, the head holds itself high, and instead of looking at our feet, we scanned the sky. The big, blue bowl of heaven pulled the sorrow right out of me, and my heart lifted like a gay balloon, and I edged a little closer to the boy next to me. He let his arm brush back and forth against mine, a little broom, sweeping away my sadness.

Lighting the Way

Dinner had been over for a long time. It had been dark outside, it seemed, forever. I returned to Grandmother's dining room once more to see if the grownups had finished their endless cups of coffee. Slipping over to the bay window behind the table, I stared out at the neighborhood lights and waited for the right moment.

In the living room the other kids were still fussing over a board game. Drowsy and a little crabby from the surfeit of good food, they seemed to have forgotten that the best part of Thanksgiving was yet to come.

I turned away from the window and leaned against my mother. "Mah-hm." "Okay, okay." My mother shifted in her chair. At last the departure had begun. I hustled importantly back into the living room. My siblings hadn't missed me, but they would pay attention now. "We're getting ready to go. Put everything away. Come on. Let's go. Come ON. We're going downtown to see the lights."

The lights. That was what Thanksgiving really meant. The turning on of the Christmas lights downtown. Before long the seven of us were packed into the car, doors slammed and locked, and then we coasted in our quiet basket from the sparse suburbs toward the worst traffic jam of the year.

As we got closer to downtown, the cars arranged themselves in long ropes, their headlights and taillights festooning the streets. I liked being one of those lights, strung out in the middle of the city dark like that, lighting the way to Christmas.

Christmas, for me, was largely a matter of lights. In the morning on the school bus, I breathed open a space in the frosted window and watched for the houses that turned on their trees for breakfast, the way I did. And at night I would go into a dark room and lean into the window, to see who in the neighborhood had remembered and who had forgotten to plug in theirs, or I would sit in our own living room with all of the other lights off and see what I could see in just the glow from the Christmas tree.

There is a special quality to that light, as though for a moment it illumines the heart of the house, the way the downtown lights illumine the heart of the city, and then, whether at home or out, for a moment we can see how rich and full light itself can be, and we are for a moment fuller and richer of heart ourselves.

Gradually the traffic slowed and then almost stopped. Downtown buildings showed themselves and finally we were on the main street itself. Ahead and overhead garlands of lights lifted in endless repetition linking building to building, street to street, and the hearts of children to each other's hearts, and the hearts of grownups to their own childhood hearts.

It was almost a relief when we reached the end of the arch and our heavy boat turned away from the stream and drifted down the long, black aisles of the other side of the city. I closed my eyes then and let myself fall asleep against the shoulders of my brothers and sisters, playing back the reel of color, of contrast, of hope against darkness.

Christmas Present

It was dark when I got up at 6:00 o'clock, and it is still dark now, at 6:30, as I back out of the garage. The headlights on the truck slap against the house and the yard, and then I am on my way, driving into the tunnel of light that I push along ahead of myself, the way humans do with their futures.

Behind me the house, that held light while I readied for this one day journey to the Cities, is dark again. Bill is asleep, and the dogs are back asleep. The fire is at rest. I stoked it, then shut it down, so the wood, yielding up its treasure slowly and evenly, will last until noon. By then Bill will be up. I will be in Minneapolis, 220 miles south.

It is too early on the road even for the school buses, but people are up. The lights in their houses glance out onto the yards, mingling with the Christmas lights they have draped on trees and around windows, extending the warmth of their living rooms and kitchens beyond the boundaries of rafters and walls.

Thirty minutes later I am snugged into the seat of a commuter airplane. As we bank around to the east and then south and set course for Minneapolis, I look down at the rows of blue and white lights held out like hands alongside the runway. Then we are above the clouds, and then I am asleep.

An hour later, I sense the plane's descent and wake up. We are below the clouds, and over the city. Street lights and freeway lights dissect the dark earth and the Mississippi River meanders right through the center of things, the way nature is wont to do. I close my eyes and focus on the pilot, sending him messages of well-being and clarity. The wheels kiss the ground, then take hold.

My sister Karen is waiting for me. She too has taken the day off, and we will spend it together. In the afternoon, she will bring me back to the airport, and I will fly home, and she will turn back onto the freeway and she will drive home. But the few hours in between are ours. We will shop and eat and gossip and laugh and reminisce, adding another strand to the braid of our history.

Downtown, we head for Dayton's, the store we grew up in. Floor by floor, the escalator lifts us. We are happy to still see the brass numbers laid into the marble at the head of each stair. We go all the way to the top, past the office floors, and up to the Sky Room, where we have lunch. Then we let the escalator take us one more time down through the stories.

Along the way we invoke memories of our mother, for that is the purpose of this day: Christmas is the season for remembering. Quieted by the long nights, we let ourselves reach back into our pasts. There we search for small candles of love, the gifts of thought and deed that outshine any package wrapped in paper. On this day downtown, Karen and I ignite again the tapers Mom left us, and for a time, the past and the present are cast in one light.

It is dark when I land in Bemidji. There is "going home" traffic on the road, and the house lights and tree lights are back on. In our living room, the fire is doing its job, and William is ready for me. I unpack my sacks, telling the tale that goes with each purchase. Then we settle back on the sofa. Bill reaches over and takes my hand, bringing me the rest of the way home.

The Finest Gifts

It is twenty-five below this morning. The fire in my office stove whistles earnestly and the smoke from the downstairs fire lifts from the chimney and then swirls back down around my second story windows as though it did not quite want to go away. The dogs bark every time a house board cracks that has been bent just as far as it is willing to go and I too sit up a little, check the fires, and make sure that we are after all secure inside this tentative wooden shell.

Cold is the touchstone for true solitude, though I cannot imagine it without its twin, the blistering white snow. Today we have both, plus the pleasure of bright sun and the absence of wind that only wants to alter things.

Yes, on a frozen day like this when even the shadows do not breathe it is easy to think that we have for a moment caught hold of time and made it stand still.

This is the perfect day, I decide, to decorate the Christmas tree. Christmas, for all its rich warmth, has a kinship to the harshest of cold: it also manages to freeze time. I pull the boxes from the shelf by the stairs, blow off the dust, and begin to unwrap the years themselves.

Each ornament has a story. As I untangle the strings and hooks I name off the people and the places. Susan and David got this in Mexico. Aaron and Andrew made these when we lived in Bowling Green. And I made these when I was fifteen. Memory, as impossible to hold onto as smoke, becomes real in these objects. I like the feel of them in my hands, and I like the way they move on the tree, turning a little in a bit of draft when someone comes in or goes out, and doing a glad dance if someone rubs almost intentionally against the tree, the way a cat walks close by a person, but seems to not really mean to touch.

In the bottom of the ornament box I come to one of my favorite treasures: a children's book of Christmas carols. It was given to the five of us by a grandmother I do not remember, and I probably would not remember the book if I had not carried it inadvertently to this place. It is illustrated with soft, angel-bestrewn water colors. There are scribbles on the inside covers, and on the back cover in bold crayon a warning: "watch out—it might be in your bed."

It is a book that got around the house. That is why the binding is loose and the pages are frayed. But what I like best about it now is that the arrangement of the carols is so easy that even I can play them correctly on the piano. A single note for the right hand, two at a time for the left. The melody emerges from behind the wooden scroll on the music ledge with the simplicity of a child's voice.

I stop decorating the tree and sit down at the piano and play and sing out loud, wrapping myself in the comfort of familiar words. Once again vague memory is given substance. I remember the year my mother asked my uncle to sing for her. He was too shy— embarrassed, even. But later, while she stood at the sink looking out at tree shadows stretched out long across the lake as though the sun in being so low on the horizon was pulling them beyond their means, he went down the bedroom hallway and into the bathroom and shut the door and began to sing.

"O Holy Night," my mother's favorite. At first only a few of us heard him, but as he gathered strength from his own voice, the words overcame the natural barriers of the walls and penetrated even the farthest rooms of the house and we fell silent and were warmed and made to shiver at the same time.

I realize that my hands have stopped moving on the keys, and that I feel both warm and a little cold. I turn back to the tree. Christmas is more than a week away, but I have already opened the finest gifts.

A Trip

It is easy to forget that it is winter back home. Rocking in a ferry boat on the San Francisco Bay, I can only think of the turbulent, grey water that cradles us. Sitting inside the glass enclosed center of the boat, I watch my son and his wife stand outside at the railing, lifting their faces up into the spray that lifts up from the boat's prow.

It is our third excursion in my one week visit. We toured the Napa Valley, tasting wine and the dank air of human-made caves. We strolled the planks of Old Town Sacramento, lingering in the aura of a past that might have been ours, but was not.

And now this trip into San Francisco. I watch Andrew and Debbie standing together in the outer air, leaning into each other, hugging and pointing to the city on the hill, to the ocean, even to the trail of birds that swarm out like a scarf in wind over our wake.

We ride that boat the way we ride our lives: Mom inside, keeping warm, the kids outside touching everything. None of us mind. We like the way we are. We have worked hard to get that way, and celebrate it in each other.

I do have a hard time, though, keeping my mouth shut. I realize how bad it is on the way home from San Francisco. I sit in the back seat, thinking I will sleep on the two hour drive. It is late afternoon and it is dark. We go from the parking lot at the wharf onto a series of freeway ramps that crawl around and over each other and then as they get free of the heart of the city, open into four lanes of traffic pouring out into what might be countryside, but is not. Because it is Friday, the entire city is leaving town. As far as we can see ahead, there are red tail lights. As far behind as we can see are headlights.

I find myself sitting straight up, my foot on an imaginary brake, my hands clenched. The line we are in becomes a steel snake. It moves steadily forward, then coils in retreat, brake lights snapping on in the opposite direction of the flow of the traffic. I start making little involuntary noises—uh—ah—oh my god! Andrew slips an old Beetles' tape into the player—some familiar comfort music for Mom. It is not enough. I fish in my pocket and find my Minnesota hat. I pull it on, and turn the rolled brim down over my eyes. After a few minutes, I begin to hear the words to the song: "Let it be, let it be."

Safe in the quiet dark of my hat, I let my hands loose and think about the trip I am on. As long as I cannot see the endless possibilities ahead of and behind me, I can enjoy the sway of the car and the gentle conversation between husband and wife in the front seat. I was right to keep quiet the times I did, to resist the desire to say "you should," and "why don't you."

"It's nice under here," I report to the front seat.

"Where?" Andrew asks.

"Under my hat," I say. "As long as I can't see those bright red brake lights coming on in a line back to us like some kind of nuclear dominoes, I don't mind being here."

"That's amazing," Andrew says. "You've pulled the wool over your own eyes."

Yes, I have. I suppose I have done it other times, when there was more behind me than I wanted to remember, and more ahead than I wanted to see. It is one way to be carried along by love.

Mittens

They're back. The lost mittens are back. And the gloves. Even the occasional hat. They are rising from the melting snow the way dreams come back to us during the day, half remembered.

I went to the feed store last week to buy taps for our maple trees. They're called spiles, actually. The feed store doesn't carry them anymore. But on the metal fence post in the parking lot, I can pick up a red mitten for free. Someone rescued it from icy mud. Someone bothered to shake it off and pull it onto the top of the fence post, sort of like dressing a child.

Yesterday I saw a glove barely hanging onto the windowsill of a downtown store. Like the mitten, it kept the memory of the hand it once warmed, its fingers curled a little.

I've done it myself—stopped in mid-stride, plucked a woolen cap from the street gutter and hung it from a "two hour parking" sign. It was an act of utter optimism. My hope must have been that the person who lost it, who was once in this place, would pass this way again. My assumption was that they still wanted the cap and that they would be grateful to my anonymous self.

It is a gratitude I've never had for someone else. First, because I have never stumbled upon any of my lost mittens. Second, if I did, I doubt that I would still have the unlost mitten, having lost it by sheer uncaring since its mate was lost. In fact, I have thrown away half a pair of mittens just so I didn't have to be reminded that I carelessly lost the other half. Still, when I see a mitten emerging from a snow bank on the side of the road, a good mitten especially, a handmade one, or a leather chopper like the one I saw last week, I want to stop the car and hang the mitten on a pussy willow branch, so it can flag down its owner and be reunited with its own kind.

No need to worry about its being stolen by someone who has no right to it. No one wants one mitten. And no one wears odd mittens. I think we know instinctively that it would be uncomfortable and even dangerous to drive a car with knitted worsted on one hand and machined acrylic on the other. Our winter-weary brains would have to sort out two sets of signals.

This is perhaps why children absolutely refuse to wear unmatched mittens. They are closer to their instincts than we are. They know that a loose fit on the left and tight fit on the right can discombobble the delicate balance required to accurately propel a snowball toward its target.

Kids of course are the ones who lose most of the mittens. It is a matter of pride with them. They'll have nothing to do with clips or strings that keep their little handwarmers handy. Maybe kids know something about mittens that we don't know. Maybe there is a mitten magnet at the center of the earth that must suck in a minimum number of mittens each winter, or the earth will lose its celestial balance.

That's it. That's why kids lose mittens, and that's why grownups don't retrieve them. In our hearts, we know that mittens have their own destinies. We resist it, sure, the way we resist our children going out on their own. Every time we pluck a mitten from oblivion, it is as useless as trying to keep our children close. No matter how many mittens we hang on parking meters, nature will have her way with this one. The mitten magnate will be fed and our children, who have always known it, will disappear from our hands as silently and as cleverly as any expensive glove. As silently and as cleverly as we did from our parents.

Memory is Egg-shaped

While the water comes to a boil, I spread newspapers out on the dining room table. I already have the coffee mugs out, each with a teaspoon of vinegar in the bottom. The bright little bottles of food coloring lie tipped over on their sides on a tray. It is time to dye Easter eggs.

My husband wants to decorate his, so I retrieve old poster paints from the craft shelf in the garage. No brushes—just a handful of Q-tips. Then these two grownups sit in the April twilight and turn eggs in colored water and set them on a wire cake rack to dry. We can't wait for that, though. Too soon we draw bold faces and flowers and fancy squiggles on the pastel backgrounds and the poster colors run together with the vinegar dye. Any child could have done it.

But there aren't any children present—just memories of them. Instead of sopping up spilled water every few minutes, I let myself wander back in memory to my own childhood: five kids scrambling around the table, squabbling over colors and eggs. Accusations fill the air: "You touched my yellow one with your blue one." "I told you to turn mine while I was gone—now it has a white spot where it stuck out of the water."

My mother is strangely absent from the memory. She must have been there, boiling the water, mopping up the spills, cooing over the wobbly designs.

I take turns rotating the two eggs I am doing, nudging them with the spoon so the water doesn't splash out, and drift into the next frame of Easter memory, the one with my children in it.

In this episode, there is still the excitement of the task, and still the accusations. I am not blamed for touching someone else's egg, but I am called to account for the quality of the raw materials: "this one is cracked" and "there aren't enough."

This year I boiled only eight eggs. Four apiece. Except I color six of them. A little bit like a kennel-raised dog that bolts its food, I move faster than I need to. My husband pokes along with his, making the lines even and using several colors on each egg. I have a brother who did that. But when my husband looks up from his work and finds that the eggs are all used, he doesn't start yelling and demanding possession of my extra eggs. Instead he watches as I turn each one in my hand, showing him how I hid the cracks with clever designs.

Then we clean up, both of us rolling up papers and carrying cups out to the sink. When we are done, I stay alone awhile in the kitchen, arranging the eggs in a basket. They still carry some of the heat from their hot water soaks. I cup each one in my hands for a moment. Memory is egg-shaped, I think. Smooth and oval and able to retain the warmth of moments gone by.

Mean Mom

My son is twenty-five. He lives in California with his wife. Awhile ago they were both sick. Someone told them to eat popsicles for fluid and for energy.

My son called me from California. "I have just bought an entire box of popsicles," he told me. "They're CHEAP. I've eaten half of them. As many as I wanted. When we were little, you only let us have one. I thought they cost a lot of money. My kids are going to have all the popsicles they want."

Yes, I was a mean mom. Once, Andrew tells me, when he was about five I sent him to his room and told him to stay there until he could tie his shoes. "I'll be here the rest of my life," he thought. I don't remember the incident, but Aaron was two at the time, and I was going to school, and Andrew was in kindergarten. I expect I had spent a goodly amount of time showing him how to tie shoelaces. I expect he wasn't very interested. I expect I really wanted to have one less thing to do in the morning.

I'm glad to know the things that Andrew is mad about. Turns out they aren't at all the things I feel guilty about. In fact, one time I decided to bare my soul to Andrew about my wrongs, to tell him how sorry I was about the time I did this and the time I didn't do that.

"What are you talking about," he said. "I don't remember any of those things. What I hated was . . .," and he recited his own list of injustices.

I had spent years wishing I had been more patient with my children when they were little. I wished I hadn't had so much to learn myself. Wished I hadn't been in such a hurry to take care of myself. Wished I hadn't yelled so much.

And now I find out that Andrew didn't like Mrs. Anderson, his after-kindergarten sitter. She made him sit on the couch and rest while she watched her favorite soap. The other children she cared for were younger, and it was their nap time. Andrew didn't understand why he couldn't go out in the yard by himself. I understood. It was Mrs. Anderson's nap time, too, the only time between 7:00 a.m. and 5:30 p.m. when she knew exactly where everyone was. Mrs. Anderson was mean all right. I liked her.

My own mother wasn't mean, that I remember. There were five of us kids, and I think she gave up control very early on. Actually, I think we were pretty mean. It wasn't until I had to drag myself upstairs one last time to put my own kids to bed that I realized what a gargantuan task that can be. Once my mother asked me to go up to tuck in my little brother. She had said she'd be up, but had forgotten. I found him under his bed, a nighttime game of hide and seek. He was asleep. I wasn't even his mother and I felt guilty. Poor little Nicky.

Not a thought for poor old Mom. I suppose I said to myself, "I'll never do that to my kids." That was a long time before I was on the other end of the good night kiss, before I went back to college and still tried to keep up with the cookie jar, before I went to work, before I got divorced.

Divorce. Now there's a neatly tied package of guilt. Whenever Andrew has a little trouble in his life, I wonder if it would be different if I hadn't been so selfish. I forget, for a moment, that I have trouble in my life and my parents weren't divorced.

And I forget why I yelled at those kids so much, but lately I've been reminded. My husband has two grandsons in grade school. We visit them now and then. They exhibit a fine decorum for about ten minutes after we arrive. Then a sort of spirit thing happens. They become Andrew and Aaron. One trips the other. The other manages to sit on a favored toy in return. Their mother offers them the great outdoors. They get as far as the hallway before they tumble back into the room crying and laughing at the same time and pulling the coat rack with them.

I wonder where I put Andrew's California phone number? I think I'll call him right now. I just remembered I have something I want to yell at him.

A Flowering

Late May, early June. Even in northern Minnesota the leaves have found their way to light, and the lilacs have opened. When I walk outside in the morning, their odor fills the yard. In the garden, the rhubarb is already trying to mature. The thick staffs of flower stalks rise from the dark green skirts of the leaves and raise tight fists of buds into the air. In the grass, creeping charlie blooms.

Our hearts too begin to blossom with the promise of summer. And although we have removed much of our daily lives from the swing of the seasons, at this time of year half of the households in the land celebrate another blossoming: graduation.

I look the word up in the dictionary. It comes from the Middle English *graduaten*, from Medieval Latin *graduare*, from Latin *gradus*, meaning step.

Tracing a word is like tracing a life: the string of connections meanders. To step: does that mean a step as in a stairway, a level, a degree? Or does it mean a step in the sense of moving forward? I look further for meaning. The appendix of the dictionary offers prehistorical word roots. Graduation leads to graduate to grade to the Indo-European root form *ghredh*, "to walk, to go."

I remember my own high school graduation. I did not like it. I did not like being dressed like everyone else. I did not like the midday sun being sucked into the black cloth of my gown. I did not want to walk into the mass of people waiting finally in the shade of the trees in the school yard.

I did not understand why I was so crabby. I had worked hard for this. Now I did not want to go, did not want to walk into the vacuum of summer.

I did not feel like a human flower about to blossom. Still, that is what happened. By August I could not wait to get away to college. Soon, I could not wait to get married, to have children. Free of the strictures of required education, I discovered the joy that goes with the onus of choosing our own experiences.

Although I graduated three times after high school, I never again participated in the formalities. Still I sought, even fought for, the degrees conferred there. And I do not dislike graduations. I have gone to many. I always cry. The tears are the same ones that come at weddings and at births and even at funerals. They are not tears of joy, or of sorrow. They are tears of overabundance. It takes water to float the mass of personal and primeval memory that we each carry into ceremony.

Next week I will attend my niece Barbara's high school graduation. I will stand next to her mother, my sister, and we will hold hands. It is for her, not for Barb, that I will drive five hours each way to sit in a crowd of people and watch a mass of silky gowns and mortar boards breath through a room big enough to hold a circus.

My sister will cry, for her daughter and for herself. I will cry for my sister and for her daughter and for myself. It is not only the students who graduate. As the child we love climbs for a brief moment into view and then descends again onto the flat playing field, every one of us will take a step forward. Afterwards we will stand outside in the weather of the season, and we will all smile the way lilacs bloom, effusively, gaudy with pleasure and filling the air with the perfume of our promise.

At the Lake

In the 1950s, we had a lake cabin thirty miles south of Minneapolis. It took an hour to get there, and as we got farther from the city, houses thinned and the road narrowed and there were farms and cows and smelly fields.

The cabin was one of a dozen or so on a dead end dirt road that separated a small wood from a point that separated two ends of the lake. We moved out in the summers as soon as school was over. For us kids much of life was the same there—we played hard and we slept well—but there were some differences. For one thing, at the lake we were allowed to read comic books. We had an orange crate full of them, and traded them with other kids from the point, and could spend all day glued to them if we wanted to. Comic books were absolutely forbidden in town.

And there was no real bedtime at the lake. I suppose this was in part because there was also no school the next morning, but I think it was more because of the nature of the point we lived on. No one came down the road who didn't live there, and at night none of us wanted to walk up the road, away from the lantern-like cabin lights, out of the trees to where corn stalks rattled in the slightest breeze.

During the day, though, we did venture away from the benign corral of our wooded-in homes. Most days, we walked the three miles round trip to the crossroad where our twisting road joined the relentless gravel roads that carved up the flat and somehow frightening fields. Our mailboxes were there, and though there was rarely anything in them, we faithfully went to look. It was, after all, something to do.

That was the blessing and the curse of summer at the lake: we could do whatever we wanted to, if we could just think of something. Our one salvation from the onus of that freedom was the Fourth of July. For that single day out of the whole summer, we knew what we would do all day and all night. It was tradition, and we were happy to be rocked in it.

It began in the morning. The dads all stayed home, even if it was mid-week. By noon, the moms had broken stride: they came out of their kitchens, bringing food with them, and sat around in each other's yards and talked and laughed and ignored their kids. Soon, the entire population of the point was gathered in two or three adjoining yards and grownups and kids wallowed in the lake and lay about on the grass and propped themselves in lawn chairs and the sun seemed to be at apogee forever.

Then, in the evening, we all ate together, carrying food away from the long tables, and strewing ourselves about the yards in little groups. The grownups drank a lot of beer and sang the sun down. Then three or four of the men slipped out onto the end of O'Toole's dock and put lit matches to the little tails that stuck out of the ends of the cardboard tubes they had set up there, and we all sat on the shore and listened for the whistle and peered out into the black sky as though if we did not pay attention we might miss the moment when human suns exploded.

Then the sky was black again. Someone broke out the sparklers and, half scared, the kids gripped them in their finger tips and over and over they tried to write their names in the air fast enough so the whole word would hang there long enough for everyone to read.

Then it was utterly dark and quiet. The kids drifted back to their cabins. The grownups stayed out awhile longer. Their voices and their songs followed us back to our beds, lullabies of summer at the lake.

A Blessing

It was their first night here. We went for a walk after dinner and by the time we got back, it was dark. But it was also warm, and we weren't ready to lock ourselves in for the night. The three of us, my son Andrew, his wife Debbie and I, stood instead in the yard and let the sky come down around us.

Andrew and I did what we always do—proudly named off the few constellations we know—and then we leaned our heads farther back and taught Debbie how to follow the curve of the outer side of the bowl of the Big Dipper and count five lengths up to find the north star.

And while we were standing there, the axis of our heads tilted like earth's, a streak of light drew itself in a line of chalk across the black sky.

Oh, we ooh'd and aah'd and then there was another and then we laid ourselves down on the grass shoulder to shoulder, the three of us, and watched shooting stars the way children watch movies, talking all the time because the human heart can sometimes not be silent in the face of wonder.

And then the loons started up, just one at first, from the bay on the other side of the point. Another called back from another bay, and then one from the lake way across the road.

We closed our eyes, still seeing stars, and the loon calls sequed into chorus and all the while I could hear my son breathing next to me, and his wife breathing next to him and no one said a word because some wonders cannot be spoken.

The blessings of that night were as an omen: all week nature's doors opened to us. Driving to town we saw a fox; a mink watched us walk the field. On the river, turtles basked and a bald eagle let us paddle back against the current and stare at him while he stared at us.

Finally he broke into flight, pumping up river, away from us, and out of sight. We drifted awhile then, the way we did so often, letting this moment or that find its place in our past.

And now the whole week is gone. Debbie and Andrew are back in California, up to their knees in city life, and I am back at my desk, watching small birds through my upstairs window. I do stop though, sometimes, and peer through the trees out to the swamp. That is where I watch the seasons change. Right now the grasses are beginning to yellow. Cattails swell with seed ready to fly. Empty, the creek bed cracks. High above us the sun glides south.

And in between migrating birds flock happily. They are going to their winter place. I imagine them there, happy in the warm sunshine, and dreaming of summer back home.

Slow Curve

They are moving our gravel washboard road. They are lifting it out of its old tired bed and straightening it and putting it down again as smooth as a ribbon pressed flat.

"When we're done, you'll be able to go fifty-five miles an hour," said the county engineer when I called to find out what was planned.

The last few nights we've walked out to the end of the driveway to see what males and machines can do in just eight hours. The slow curve we live on is still intact and for the moment our mailbox, across the road from the drive, keeps its place, holding steady in an eliptical oasis of brome grass.

Just on the other side of it, the earth movers have been at work. During the day we listen to them slogging back and forth, hauling dirt up into their heavy bellies and belching it back out in some other place.

We stand next to our mailbox in the long evening light and marvel at the sight before us. There is so much more to earth than it looks like from on top. The machines have cut a canyon fifty feet wide and twenty feet deep and running as far as we can see to left and right, sometimes touching, sometimes leaping away from the old road. Farthest from us are the black rolls of top soil that once were field. Then, down the slope, long strands of caramel sand, and farther down, ropes of darker sand, and woven through it all braids of roots and gravel and humus and odd twists of color that I do not understand.

I have felt out of balance all day. The post lady cannot get through, so I do not have today's mail, and the letters I put in the box this morning are still there, the red flag holding its salute.

And tonight, standing on the brink of progress, my husband and I both feel a little lost. The few pickups that usually beat their way home on this path are going the long way around to come in at the north end. The gargantuan green and yellow machinery that chortles all day is silent now, but is parked in neat rows, front to end, front to end, and seems only to be holding its breath.

What is it like, I wonder, to drive a machine like that? Sometimes I wave to the men. They wave back from their little glass boxes perched on top of the engines that push and pull the steel caterpillar tracks. I like to watch them. They ride that equipment the way men ride horses, their torsos upright, their hips rocking with the machines.

Sometimes I see them eating their lunches. They climb down from their metal steeds and pick and lurch their way across the roils of earth and sit in a row in the shade of the woods, their backs to the trees. Even from far away you can see the fatigue in their shoulders.

By summer's end the road will be fixed. Our driveway will be longer. It will step over the old path and hitch up with the new, with its unruffled spine and wide sweeping berms. And when we turn onto it we will yield to the lure of the straight-away: we will speed. There will be no curves to hide deer leaping from one wood to the next. No mud holes betraying the life of underground springs. No mallards taking flight from damp ditches. Just a stretch of standardized highway pulling us headlong out of the twentieth century.

On the Way to Town

It is an overcast and misty day. Although it is noon, the air has the feeling of twilight. Maybe that is why the deer are on the road when they should be resting in the woods.

I am also not where I am supposed to be, in reality driving down the road at fifty-five miles an hour. But my head, or my heart, is elsewhere, lulled by the softness of the humid air and the gentleness of the light.

I do not see the deer until I am nearly on them. There are three. They are standing in the middle of my lane, heads turned toward me.

I am able to stop the car in time, although I do not expect to. To my surprise, the brakes do not squeal, or if they do I do not hear them. And more to my surprise, as I stare out the windshield at the deer staring at me, I realize my right arm is extended out across the passenger seat.

The deer get bored and trundle off into the ditch and then bounce into the woods, leaving me stopped in the middle of the highway, with my arm sticking out as though pointing the way to somewhere.

I give up the salute, shift into first gear, and resume my trip, this time distracted not by day dreams but by the sheer wonder of the moment just passed.

I could easily have been killed had I connected physically with those deer, but I did not. And the deer are safe too, browsing in the woods that still follow alongside the road.

I replay the event. I don't recall when I first saw the deer. My consciousness of them comes after I started to brake.

And I think that came after I threw my arm out across the passenger seat. I know why I did that. I learned it from my mother, who did it, and it became instinct, if that is possible, from repetition with my own two children. When there is danger, or the possibility of danger, the arm goes out to hold them back. To keep the children on the seat.

The arm swings out from the mother, the way a gate comes down at a railroad crossing, tripped by the flying assault of the engine before the cars on the road can see it or hear it.

My siblings and I used to get mad at Mom. Even when we were teenagers that arm would come out when the brake went on. And I did it to my sons, and they said what we said: "Mahhhh-mmm, really."

Andrew is twenty-seven years old and lives in California with his wife, but today I reached out to save him. Three deer stepped out of the mist as though they were stepping out of history, and made me remember what I cannot forget. Now they are gone, and I am back on my way to town. It was just a few odd moments in an ordinary morning. Still, it has slowed me down.

Tomatoes

I had breakfast with a friend the other day—another writer. She had received a grant to do poetry, but was lamenting a sad fact: there was no time for poems. She had to can tomatoes.

No matter that she had never canned tomatoes before in her life. Even her mother didn't can tomatoes. But this fall she had to do it. She had grown them herself, and they called to her from the garden like lost children.

When I was there, she already had two dozen quarts lined up along the back of the kitchen cupboard, as though they had to be watched. She held one up to the window, tipped it a little to one side and smiled as the morning sun found its way through the golden red pulp. Then she set it back down on the cupboard and tucked it in close to the others.

I know how it is. I have twenty-four pints of rhubarb butter gracing the shelves on my basement stairway.

We went out to eat. Kathy was worried about the grant. The poems were backed up in her head and her heart, waiting for the door to open that would let them spill out into the basket of white paper. It was a harvest of its own kind.

But the tomatoes, she knew, would not wait. I know, I said, and told her about the rhubarb butter. Of course, we agreed, winter would be different—long strands of solitude to braid into ropes of verse and prose. Then we would get things done.

By this time in our conversation both of us knew the real value in fall canning. It is an air-tight alibi for not facing a blank page. Some people think they are not writers because it is so hard for them to get started, but caution is wise when you are entering unexplored lands. Hidden in the packed white fibers of blank paper are cliffs, and pits, and long barren plains where a heart can wander and get lost and finally disappear. And valleys and meadows and limpid ponds of hope and love are just as likely. You see how a few words can change the landscape. We are right to hesitate before closing our eyes and stepping into that dream.

No matter how many gardens we do preserve, in the end, winter will out, and perhaps we count on that. It comes the way sleep does, predictably, and lays before us a white sheet of possibility. Even a single black crow thumbing its way across the sky seems to have something to say then.

Kathy and I lingered that morning over cups of tea. After awhile we didn't talk about writing anymore, at least not directly. Our words found roads into the long reaches of heart we had separately explored in the twenty years since we first met.

By the time we left, we were both anxious to get home to our desks. Talking out loud like that, strands of poems escaped into the air. They called to us like lost children. Encouraged, given courage, by each other's pasts, we hurried away into long fields of paper, where we could call out and wait for the echo back.

Election

Out in rural Puposky, where I live, human history is easy to observe. From my office window I look out over a floating bog. A creek winds its way, like thought, from one end to the other. Now that it is nearly winter and the canary grass has burned itself into the ground, I can see again the fence posts that walk from our south line out to the creek.

At one time the posts were joined by wire, and sheep grazed on the lush summer grasses. Things were different then. Even humans could cross the bog and there was a ford in the creek that led to Grandma's house on the other side of the swamp.

I learned this from the man who grew up here. He was raised and raised his family in the log cabin that is our living room. He told me too about the old tote road that went through this place. I can still see the rutted tracks down at the other end of the field.

And he told me about the town of Puposky—its school and its stores. They are gone now, but I still go there for two things: the post office and the Durand Township hall. These are my links to the larger society I live in. Without the post office, I would have only myself to write to. Without the township hall, I would have nowhere to vote.

Nowhere to vote. Actually, I am amazed that I do have a place to vote. I am a lazy person. I don't wash my windows, I don't sweep my floors, and I have never waxed a car. I don't think I'd go to the trouble of organizing a nationwide network for counting people's dreams. When I am in the township hall voting, I am amazed even that it is there, out in the middle of the swamps and trees. But there it is, and it has electricity, and heat, and old leather bound books with hand-written records in them.

I do not think about these images except when I go to the hall to vote. Then the smells and sounds and little touches of human caring gather like clouds and remind me that I am a lucky person. I begin to feel both patriotic and a little corny. Many people did die to establish this democracy. Others, still today, give up their time and spend their energy doing the minute chores that keep it going. In my polling place, several women and men spend a whole day and a good part of an evening waiting for people like me to bother to come in and vote. Sometimes there are fewer than a dozen of us.

Each time I go there, my footsteps echo against the bare walls. The folks at the table at the head of the room watch me approach. We smile and nod at each other. Someone looks my name up in the incongruous computer print-out and checks it off. Someone else hands me my ballots. I step up onto the little stage, walk past the two padlocked ballot boxes with their dark mouths that wait for my return.

I step inside one of the two voting booths, partitioned-off corners of the stage. A sagging curtain implies privacy. Inside on a wooden shelf attached to the wall are several pencils. They are nailed there via pieces of white string stuck to the pencil erasers with common pins.

This is so simple, I think to myself. A few slips of paper. A pencil. And all I have to do is make my mark—my X—the sign in our society of an individual. It takes me less than a minute. I fold the papers, return to the main room, and poke them into the proper boxes.   For some reason   I think of the fence posts marching across the swamp at home.   Suddenly I cannot tell if they lead forward or back. And I cannot tell if I have made history today, or if history has made me.

Desert Storm, 1991

It is a perfect afternoon for cross country skiing. The temperature is mild: twenty degrees above zero. The wind is not too strong. The sky is bright, though not quite cloudless.

Dragging our skis and poles behind us, Helen and I trudge through the yard snow over to the crest of the hill, then make our way down, climbing over trees felled by last summer's storms. There we balance ourselves in the drifts tossed up from the lake and hitch our boots to our skis, their slick bottoms squeaking in the snow as we shift from one foot to the other.

There are three other noises I am aware of as I stand up straight and breathe in the solitude of the swamp. Off to my right is a small wood where the branches of oaks and maples rub against each other, creaking with the cold.

To my left, a pileated woodpecker works at the heart of an elm tree. Once he was called the lord god woodpecker, maybe because he just goes about his business and lets the humans do what they will. With his bill he taps the white inner wood of the tree, a knocking of sorts.

Ahead of me is the swamp and the canary grass that we must get through to get to the bay. The tops of the slender leaves, standing taller than the snow, still winnow the wind, rubbing out a very quiet song.

And all around is the cerulean sky. It has no sound. Makes no noise. Mute. The sky is mute. I had not thought of that before. And if that is true, what is it in the sky that makes me wonder what time it is right now half the world away? It would be dark, of course. What about the wind? What about birds? What about the forests? Somewhere where I am not, do tree branches wring their hands for the heat?

Helen and I move out. I lead, laying down the trail that will later bring us back to home. I had forgotten what hard work that can be. The heat of the swamp has kept the snow melted from underneath, and with every step I take, my foot and leg drops down into the tangled mane of last year's grasses. I stop often to breathe, and to peer down into the fist-sized holes that dot the snow. Frost rims the dark throats of these vents that lead to deep-rooted springs that even during the intractable winter percolate beneath us.

Then we are at the white desert of the lake. The hill and the woods seem far away. Even the sky seems to have pulled back, and a small airplane off to the south, looping in lazy, friendly lines, drones in its own world. The wind, though, is more present. A splash of red rises to my cheeks.

Now we can make time. Helen comes alongside, and we stretch with our legs and torsos and arms and ride over the crystalline snow, packed hard by the prevailing westerlies.

What is it this time that breaks in? Suddenly I remember the weeks and months after my son Aaron died. I would wake in the morning from a bad dream. At first I could not remember what it was, and then I would remember that I had dreamed that Aaron had died. "What a horrible dream," I would say to myself. And then I would wake up some more and would remember that it was not a dream. Aaron was dead.

Helen and I are skimming now across the lake, the momentum of our bodies pulling us into our personal futures. How good it feels to glide like this, almost free of the earth. I swallow the wind. My eyes give in to the sun on the snow: I do not see where I am going. And all I can hear is the palpitating beat of a heart hard at work. It is not mine, though. It is coming to me from somewhere else. From half way around the world. How can this be? Am I dreaming?

Plants

The Christmas cactus is ready to bloom. Its magenta buds hold themselves out from the leaf stalks, shimmering with anticipation. A few have started to open. Their golden stamins and the pistils leap out from the cradle of their white throats.

Taking a deep breath, I lift the pot that is heavy with soil and history and carry it downstairs. Its three foot spread of branches and blossoms mingles with my hair and as we enter warmer air I am swathed in the smell of earth's produce.

This cactus sets buds according to rules laid down long ago— cool air, short light, but it has human memories as well. It started from a cutting from Roger. His plant is more than fifty years old, started by an aunt. I like having this progeny growing in my house, roots that reach beyond the clay of the pot into the common soil of the past.

All of my plants have a personal history. All have a parent plant in another household. The *ficus* I got during a visit to Judith. Three of the cacti are from Andrew's California apartment. Two are from my dad's Florida home. One *mammalaria* is from Marion, another from Shirley. The burro's tail—from Danna.

I am attracted to succulents. They live for long lengths of time on their own juices, the way a writer should be able to. They are strong enough to carry the tangle of memory that I attach to each one, their idiosyncratic growth echoing the spirit of the person they stand for. And sometimes they betray a deeper life. The serpentine cactus from my father's grows like Ophelia's hair and has taken over a south window. Last year it startled us with a blossom, white, rank, bigger than a man's hand. It erupted one evening, was done by midnight; we had been visited.

I place the Christmas cactus on a stand across the room from the Christmas tree. In between, on a low table, a handful of dried milkweed stalks holds out glossy pods. On the wall, a drawing of a grapevine brings summer into sight. And all along the window sills, pots of earth keep faith with the sun, each one sending up the light of an immortal green messenger.

A Blue Bird Am I

When I first started making the walk to Barbie Egekvist's, it was a long way to go. I was eight, or nine. Once a week, after school, I went there to Blue Birds. Out the back door, cut across the yard to the corner of Emerson and 73rd. Right on 73rd to Oak Grove. Left on Oak Grove to Barbie's house, the sixth one down.

Two blocks, in all, past large frame houses framed with yards full of old oaks and elms and maples. I didn't mind the part on 73rd. Lottielee's house was in sight the whole time. But I got nervous when I made the turn onto Oak Grove. It went straight for two houses and then curved right. Lottielee's house disappeared from sight before Barbie's came into view, and a few doors past Barbie's house the street curved again and disappeared into a canopy of leaves.

I'd never been past Barbie's. You didn't always know what could happen to you in the fringes of your own neighborhood. One time, on my tricycle, I wasn't paying attention and pedaled myself clear up Emerson and along 74th and then up another street. I didn't know I was lost until the resident kids came out. They surrounded me with their trikes and wanted to know what I was doing there. I tried to turn around and leave, but they wouldn't let me go, and

I cried and a mom came out and freed me and walked me down to 74th and pointed up the street to show me which one of the corners to turn at to get back home.

Each week, on my way to Blue Birds, when I turned onto Oak Grove, I counted the houses up to Barbie's. Her mom would let me in, and I went through the living room and the kitchen and down the basement stairs and through Mr. Egekvist's workshop to a long, white room, and joined the other girls, who also wore navy blue skirts and vests and white blouses and little red neck bows and blue caps.

We settled into a circle and opened our meeting with song: "A Blue Bird am I, and some day I'll fly, then a Camp Fire Girl I'll be." I had an image of myself expanding to the size of a young woman and sprouting wings and taking off. From the air there would be no secrets and home would be easy to find.

The successful and weekly venture down Oak Grove eventually eroded the memory of the tricycle tragedy, and by the time I flew up and became a Camp Fire Girl, I had walked many times past the house with the red steps. And I had biked even farther, clear across Lyndale Avenue, to the library.

But I still didn't like propelling myself away from home, so I sang as I pedaled along, not only Blue Bird and Camp Fire Girl songs, but ones I had learned at camp and at church. The lyrics carried for me the comfort of the known and I pumped them out to the rhythm of my heart. As my ventures gradually included friends farther away and then schools and stores and theaters, the tunes were a track that I could follow back whenever I felt too far from the hearth.

I even counted sometimes the houses on the street I was traveling, as though that could keep me from going too far. And still today I hold back once in a while when I see a curve in the road. I close my eyes then and try to fly ahead of myself and see just where I am in relation to home.

Close Around Me

It is overcast this morning. Although the sun is up and about, its signature of light scrawled across the land, there is no sign of the disc itself.

The clouds that so perfectly hide the sun seem not to be clouds at all. There are no ripples. No waves. No strands of celestial hair. No swatches of blue. There is only a monotone shroud that is neither grey nor white. And although it is early morning, it is just as light in the west as in the east, some trick of refraction that is beyond my understanding of heavens.

When my son Andrew was about twelve, he decided to learn to play the harmonica. He spent a weekend, then a week channeling his breath into the tiny holes allotted for each note. One day he came down from his room and slumped over the kitchen counter. "The world takes too much practice," he declared.

That is how I feel this morning, with the sky so blank, and all the possibility of the rest of my life spread out in a circle around me. Which way do I go on this day, December 24th, my birthday?

I wish I knew more about the day of my birth. I think I was born around five in the afternoon. I think there was supposed to be a gathering at my parents' house that evening, but I intervened.

I think my mother must not have cared. I have a picture of her holding me the day I came home from the hospital. We are outside, in front of the house. Maybe because the picture is old, and black and white, or maybe because that is the way it was, it looks like an overcast day. My mother is happy. With one hand, she pulls the blanket away just enough to reveal my face. Her own face bends down, a mirror of sorts.

She placed a song in my name: Susan Carol, because I was born on Christmas Eve. It was the first of many blessings that were accidents of my birth.

It was my mother's women friends who told me I was special because of the day I was born on. In the end, I had four siblings, two ahead of me, two behind. I was the only one who got birthday presents from all of my mother's friends.

They remembered the day I was born. During the holiday week, they delivered unto me little gifts. They did not want my birthday to get lost in the confusion of presents given to just anyone. They bent down close to me, whispered, as though this were some kind of secret transaction. "You are special," they would say.

I must have believed it. I remember my brothers and sisters' disgust. I remember gloating because I got to open presents on Christmas Eve, and no one else did. That was, I suppose, one of my mother's tricks for keeping the day special for me. It worked. There is nothing more special than having a sure fire edge on your brothers and sisters.

They seem to have forgiven me. All day today my phone will ring, and I will be sung to. Friends will call, too. It is easy to remember a Christmas Eve birthday. And maybe life is easier when you grow up being whispered to that you are special. It keeps me warm, a shawl of sorts. On overcast days, I draw it close around me.

The Ride

Grey sky. Snow begins to appear in the air, as though it had been there all the time, but only now is visible. It does not seem to come from somewhere else and is not attracted to the ground. Instead it wafts around the yard, the way children play in the afternoon—lazing about for awhile, then suddenly colliding with each other in a momentary frenzy.

January is the fulcrum of winter. The thermometer holds steady in the cold zone. Snow does not melt, or accumulate. Winter is not coming on, nor is it going away. At my desk, looking out onto the still life of the swamp, only my thoughts are able to wander, and even they are suspended in the season.

I remember a hayride. When I was in grade school, we lived across the street from a lake. There was a skating rink and warming house on the other side and on weekends there were hayrides. The long plank wagon was pulled by two horses. From the neighbor's yard we watched them bumping along their snowy track.

We wanted to ride on that wagon, but how to convince our parents? There was a gang of us in on this project, including some older brothers and sisters. They figured it out: if we only needed a ride one way, maybe we could finagle a ride over. Then we could jump off the sleigh as it passed in front of our shore and walk back home— a sort of matching energy grant.

The gambit worked. The older ones were reprimanded in advance in case they didn't take proper care of the younger ones, and our bundled bodies were dropped off in the skating rink parking lot.

I don't remember getting on the sleigh, or even the ride around the north and west sides of the lake. My consciousness comes into focus as we curved toward the south shore. I hadn't realized how far away from land the track actually was. The houses looked small and remote, as though they belonged to other people, not to us. And suddenly the sleigh was going awfully fast and the runners propelled themselves across the snow without mercy.

The bigger kids began to organize us. We lined up along the shore-side of the planks. One of the smaller children began to cry a little. Other kids heard what we were going to do and everyone watched. Some of us jumped. Some of us were shoved or pulled off. And somehow, one of us was left behind. We shouted and jumped around as she pulled away from us like time itself, her arms held out toward us, her legs paralyzed.

By this time the driver was onto us. He drew up the horses. The sleigh stopped. He was furious and we had a hard time to convince him that we had parental approval. Someone pulled the chicken kid off into the snow and we all stood and watched the horses and the sleigh and the other children and the grownup glide off into the white afternoon.

The snow between us and the houses was deep and soft, not like the trail packed hard by the horses. Our pilgrimage bogged down before it got started. We literally could not move. The older ones tried to make a path, but they only made more holes to fall into. I knelt on the snow. My fingers were stiff and cold. I could not feel my feet. The sun dazzled in my eyes and I could not see. That is when I learned that death wears white.

I wonder how it looked to the grownups watching from the nearest house—a dozen bright young bodies blazing in the winter sun. I wonder when they knew that we were in trouble. One of the dads came out to us then on snow shoes. He packed a waffled track and we crawled it on our hands and knees not daring at first to stand and then got up one at a time and carried ourselves home.

And then my mother was rubbing my toes, white as a dead man's. I was safe. I was beginning to get warm. The pain was going away. But I did not stop crying.

White Wings

This has been a good, strong winter. I walk slowly down the driveway, admiring the crisp, tall banks of snow that rise up on each side. Parted by the force of a good plow, they allow me to exit my dwelling and to reach the mailbox. I cross the road carefully. The packed snow has melted and frozen and remelted onto itself and is as slippery as memory.

But the past does not interest me at this moment. I feel a familiar breeze of hope in my heart as I take off my mitten and pull down the mailbox door.

What is waiting for me? Because I am a writer, I have two primary expectations: acceptances and rejections, the same dichotomy we face one way or another almost every hour of our days. Big, brown envelopes addressed to me in my own hand mean my words have found their way back to me—messenger pigeons of the heart.

Acceptances come in small dove white envelopes, addressed to me by some unknown hand, and hide themselves in the slender stack of first class mail that tops a stack of catalogs and fliers.

That handful of small white missives is the one I care about. I skate back across the road and let my feet find their own way back to the house. Pinched lightly in my left hand, the catalogs and brown envelopes make a cradle for the smaller, more delectable fare. I flip the envelopes forward one at a time, scanning the upper left corner for clues to their origins.

I wonder sometimes why I have such faith in the mailbox when it has disappointed me so many times. It has even, maybe especially, failed me when I needed it the most, at the end of a long day of little failures. I'll have been kicking around the kitchen, dropping and spilling things when I remember that I have not gone out for the mail. It always feels good then to get outside, into air unstirred by small emotions. I'll walk deliberately down the drive, watching the trees for birds or following a cloud in its journey across the sky.

Nature never fails me, but the mailbox is a human device. A bill. A catalog of things I don't want. A sweepstakes notice of my probable impending wealth.

Nothing. I shuffle back to the house, kicking small things that have lit in the tire rut. I remember the year a long time ago when I was newly married, and my husband was job hunting. Every day on my way out to the mailbox I uttered an internal prayer, as though the little metal house itself could somehow conjure up our future.

I know better now, but luck and love have cooperated often enough to still let me hope and, inevitably, at some time one letter I am always ready for is there. It is not from a publisher offering fame or a publishing house offering fortune. It is a letter from a friend with a few notes on the weather in another place and time. A little gossip maybe about the children, or a book that should be read. Wishes that we could sit together over a cup of tea and watch the birds at the window feeder.

At the kitchen table, I fill my cup, release the folded pages from their casing and read them again and again. When I was a Camp

Fire girl I learned a song: "White wings that never grow weary, that carry me cheerily over the sea. Night falls, I long for thee dearly, I spread out my white wings, and sail home to thee." I didn't understand. All my friends were with me, sitting in a circle. Our troop leader asked what the white wings might be. Dreams, someone thought. A letter, said someone else: "white wings that never grow weary." I close my eyes and imagine my friend sitting here with me. The white sheets of her letter flutter in my hands.

Susan Hauser resides in Puposky, Minnesota. She is a free-lance writer, essayist and poet. Her commentaries are heard regularly on KCRB public radio, Bemidji, Minnesota. *Meant To Be Read Out Loud* (Loonfeather Press), the first collection of her KCRB commentaries, received a 1989 Minnesota Book Award (Minnesota category). She earned a Master of Fine Arts degree in poetry from Bowling Green State University, Ohio, in 1973.

Roger Winters is a self-taught artist who began painting in the early 1950s. He works in a variety of media including pen and ink, collage, and colored pencil. Recently his work was shown at the Judith Stern gallery in Minneapolis.